HAMID'S STORY

A Real-Life Account of His Journey from Eritrea

Editor: Michelle Hasselius
Production Specialist: Tori Abraham
The illustrations in this book were created digitally.

Picture Window Books are published by Capstone,
1710 Roe Crest Drive, North Mankato, Minnesota 56003
www.mycapstone.com

Library of Congress Cataloging-in-Publication Data
Library of Congress Cataloging-in-Publication data is available on the
Library of Congress website.
ISBN 978-1-5158-1413-9 (library binding)
ISBN 978-1-5158-1418-4 (eBook PDF)

Glossary

journey (JUR-nee)—a long trip

Red Sea (RED SEE)—a long,
narrow sea that separates the
Arabian Peninsula from northeastern Africa

border (BOR-dur)—the dividing line between
one country or region and another

street market (STREET MAR-kit) a place where
people buy and sell food or goods; street
markets are usually outdoors and often, but
not always, in a street

HAMID'S STORY

A Real-Life Account of His Journey from Eritrea

by Andy Glynne

illustrated & designed by Tom Senior

PICTURE WINDOW BOOKS

a capstone imprint

My name is Hamid. This is the story of my journey from Eritrea.

When my family and I were living in Eritrea, it was always hot and busy.

There were lots of street markets in our town.
At the markets people sold different kinds of food.

It was so hot at the markets,
the food had flies swarming
all over it.

The streets were dusty.
When the wind blew,
I would end up with lots
of dust in my eyes.

Eritrea is a small country in Africa, but lots of people live there. The buses were always packed full. We usually had to stand, because there weren't enough seats for everyone.

Even babies had to give up their seats to older people. It could be very dangerous for the babies.

A long time ago, Eritrea was a big country. Then the land was divided between Eritrea and Ethiopia.

Eritrea's northern border was next to the Red Sea.

A war started because
Ethiopia wanted access
to the Red Sea.

The Eritrean people wanted to escape the war. But it was hard to get a flight out of the country.

Many people fled Eritrea. They wanted to find a safe home for themselves and their families.

My dad knew secrets about the Eritrean government. The officials said if he told anyone these secrets, they would kill my mom and me!

My dad told us we had to run
away. He couldn't come with us,
because the government wouldn't
let him leave the country.

My mom and I boarded a plane.
All I can remember is that we
traveled for a very, very long time.

For part of our journey, we took
a bus. I slept a lot of the way.

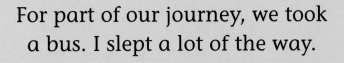

Finally we arrived in our new country.
It was really difficult for us at first, because
we didn't speak the language.

I started school. It was scary, because
I didn't have any friends. The other
kids already had groups of friends.

One day on the playground, a boy asked me if we could be friends. We started playing together. After a little while, we joined in with lots of other kids.

Soon we made a new group of friends.

A few weeks later, I arrived home from school to find lots of people in my house. Everyone was crying.

I went upstairs to my mom's room, and she was sitting on the bed.

"I have something to tell you," she said. "Your dad died back home in Eritrea."

We both got really upset. After a little
while, we told each other that we had
to be strong and stop crying. So we did.

For a few days, I could hardly eat anything. I drank a little bit of water but couldn't finish my lunch at school.

The next day my mom spoke to me.

She explained that I shouldn't be so upset.
The reason we left Eritrea was because it
was so dangerous.

I began to feel much better after our talk.
I realized it was a good thing that we left
Eritrea and came to this new country.

I've made a lot of new
friends. We don't talk
about our lives at home.
We act like sad things have
never happened to us.

When I'm feeling sad, my friend tells me a joke and cheers me up. And when he's feeling sad, I tell him a joke and cheer him up. Life is much better for my mom and me now.